...............Contents...............

Introduction . . .2
Features 5
Assessment . . .7

Unlocking Analogies 2–3, SV 9781419033902

What Are Analogies?

Analogies show relationships between words. Working with analogies helps students build critical-thinking and reasoning skills that will help them in their everyday learning and also on standardized tests. Students are encouraged to be creative and think outside the box, strengthening their thinking skills across the school curriculum and helping them in their other life activities.

Working with analogies also encourages students to

- expand their vocabulary.
- understand the relationships between words and ideas.
- recognize different meanings for words.
- read more carefully.

Students can apply the skills they learn through analogies to other school subjects as well as to other areas of life.

How to Read Analogies

Students are exposed to a variety of formats in which analogies can be given. Each format is explained both when it is introduced and when it reoccurs. Pictures are used to introduce each new concept. Key words in the explanations and exercises are underlined or placed in boldface type in order to reinforce their importance to the analogy. Encountering analogies in different formats helps students become more comfortable with making comparisons between words and reinforces the information by showing it in slightly different ways.

> **A shark is a type of fish**, and a cow is a **type of mammal.**
>
> <u>Shark</u> is to <u>fish</u> as <u>cow</u> is to <u>mammal</u>.
>
> shark : fish :: cow : mammal

The symbols used in analogies (: and ::) are explained in several different units. The single colon (:) is read as "is to." The double colon (::) is read as "as." Thus, happy : cheerful :: sad : glum is read as

Happy *is to* cheerful *as* sad *is to* glum.

How to Use the Book

Breaking down analogies into different types helps students become comfortable with one type of analogy before they are ready to explore another. Students gradually encounter more types of analogies and identify what comparison is being made between the words. Each unit also provides different formats for looking at analogies: multiple choice, matching, and fill in the blank, as well as pictures versus words. Each unit starts with picture activities to provide a visual connection with the type of analogy being presented. Once students are comfortable making comparisons with pictures, they can transition smoothly into making analogies with words.

All materials can be reproduced and distributed to students to work individually, as partners, or in small groups.

How to Introduce Students to Types of Analogies

Unit 1: Shapes and Pictures (pages 8 to 11)

In order to work successfully with analogies, students must understand how to categorize words. At this age level, students may feel more comfortable working with pictures first. Students are asked to identify similarities between shapes or pictures that make them part of the same group.

Demonstrate the skill:

① Show students a variety of pictures of animals: cat, dog, horse, pig, fish, mouse. Include some different types of each animal (dog: golden retriever, dachshund, pug; fish: goldfish, catfish, carp) and pictures of animals at different life stages (cat, kitten; pig, piglet; horse, colt).
② Ask students what these pictures have in common. (They are all types of animals.)
③ Ask students to identify different ways to group these animals (pets, barnyard animals, breeds of one type of animal, family groups, etc.).
④ Lead students to find different ways to group other items.
⑤ Introduce the analogy format:

_____ is to _____ as _____ is to _____

Unit 2: Similarities (pages 12 to 16)

After grouping items in Unit 1, students can now begin to understand how similar items are related to each other. They can also begin to compare items in one group to items in another.

Demonstrate the skill:

① Show students pictures of a robin, a parrot, a bulldog, and a poodle. Write the words *robin*, *parrot*, *bulldog*, and *poodle* on the board.
② Ask students to look at the pictures and tell how a robin and a parrot are alike. (They are both types of birds.) Ask students to look at the pictures and tell how a bulldog and a poodle are alike. (They are both types of dogs.)
③ Ask students to explore other ways that things can be alike, such as part of the same group or where they are found.

Unit 3: Part to Whole (pages 17 to 22)

Unit 3 introduces students to the concept of part-to-whole relationships. An important type of analogy is one that compares parts to a whole.

Demonstrate the skill:

① Discuss part-to-whole relationships with students. Show students a picture of a face and write the following words on the board: *eyes, nose, mouth, ears*. Ask students what these words are part of. (*face* or *head*)
② Have students name other wholes that can be divided into parts and draw pictures of them.
③ Introduce the analogy format:

   Finger is to hand as toe is to foot.
④ Discuss how to interpret the analogy: A finger is part of a hand, and a toe is part of a foot.
⑤ Introduce students to the symbols used in analogies (: and ::) and continue the comparison using the analogy symbols.

   finger : hand :: toe : foot
⑥ Point out that if the first pair of words are parts of a whole, then the second pair of words must be parts of a whole as well. However, all the words do not have to be related to each other or be parts of the *same whole*.
⑦ Also emphasize that the order of words in analogies is important.

Unit 4: User to Object (pages 23 to 28)

Unit 4 introduces students to the concept of user-to-object relationships.

Demonstrate the skill:

① Discuss user-to-object relationships with students. Show students a picture of a construction worker and ask them to name tools he or she uses (hammer, saw, wrench, screwdriver). Write the names of the tools on the board and ask students to draw pictures of them.
② Have students name other jobs people have and the kinds of tools they use to do their work. Students can choose a job and illustrate it along with the tools needed.
③ Introduce the use of user-to-object relationships in analogies. Point out that if the first pair of words are a user and an object, then the second pair of words must be a user and an object as well. However, all the words do not have to be related to each other.

   Bicycle rider is to bike as swimmer is to pool.

Unit 5: Synonyms (pages 29 to 34)

In Unit 5, students are introduced to the concept of synonyms, words that are similar in meaning to each other.

Demonstrate the skill:

① Discuss synonyms with students. Show students pictures of some things that are *hot* (fire, sun, stovetop). Ask them to think of as many words that mean the same thing as *hot* as they can (*warm, fiery, burning*). Record their answers on the board.
② Ask students to choose an adjective, draw pictures of things that represent it (*tall:* man, skyscraper, tree), and name other adjectives that could be used to describe the pictures (*giant, big, high*).
③ Introduce the use of synonym pairs in analogies. Point out that if the first pair of words are synonyms, then the second pair of words must be synonyms as well. However, all the words do not have to be synonyms for each other.

   Hot is to warm as cold is to cool.

3

Unit 6: Antonyms (pages 35 to 40)

Unit 6 introduces students to the concept of antonyms, words that mean the opposite of each other.

Demonstrate the skill:

① Discuss antonyms with students. Show students pictures of some things that are *hot* (fire, sun, stovetop). Then ask them to think of as many words that mean the opposite of *hot* as they can. Record their answers on the board.

② Ask students to draw pictures of things that are opposites (summer/winter, tall/short, light/dark) and write the words associated with them.

③ Introduce the use of antonym pairs in analogies. Point out that if the first pair of words are antonyms, then the second pair of words must be antonyms as well.

<u>Hot</u> is to <u>cold</u> as <u>warm</u> is to <u>cool</u>.

Unit 7: Name and Description (pages 41 to 46)

In Unit 7, students are introduced to the concept of analogies using names and descriptions. In order to understand this type of analogy, students must be comfortable using nouns and adjectives.

Demonstrate the skill:

① Show students pictures of animals (sheep, giraffe, chick). Ask students to name words that describe the animals (sheep: *woolly;* giraffe: *tall;* chick: *downy*). Discuss with students the difference between nouns (names of animals) and adjectives (words that describe the animals).

② Have students draw another animal and list words to describe it. Ask them to identify the noun (naming word) and adjectives (describing words).

③ Introduce the type of analogy that uses names and descriptions. Point out that if the first pair of words give a name and a description, then the second pair of words must also give a name and a description.

<u>Elephant</u> is to <u>big</u> as <u>mouse</u> is to <u>small</u>.

·-·-·-·-·-·-·-·-· Features ·-·-·-·-·-·-·-·-·

Assessment

The **Assessment** at the beginning of the book can be used to test students before and after studying analogies.

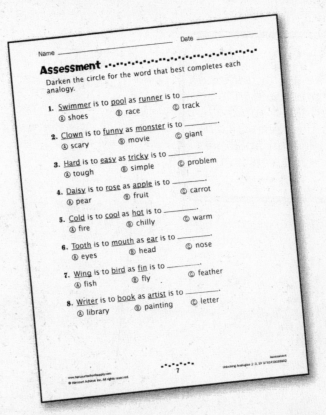

The **Key to Solving** box at the beginning of each lesson provides an example of how to understand the exercises in that lesson.

Lesson Page

Each lesson page provides **explicit instruction** in how to analyze and interpret analogies.

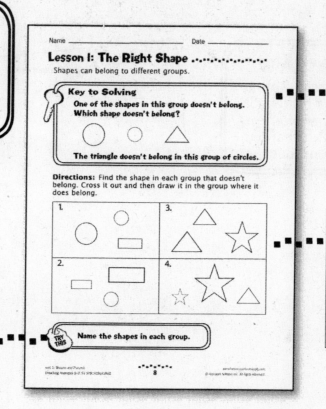

The activities are in multiple **formats**, using both words and pictures: multiple choice, matching, and fill in the blank.

The **Try This** activity at the end of each lesson provides additional practice in working with the type of analogy presented in that unit.

Unlocking Analogies 2–3, SV 9781419033902

Review Page

The analogies are presented in a scaffolded approach, and the reviews cover all types of analogies introduced until that point.

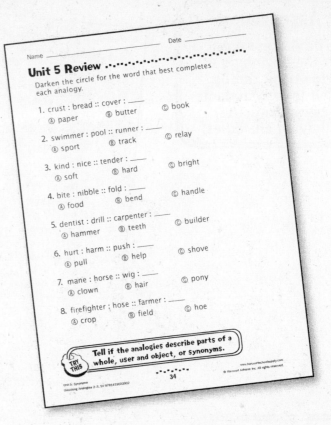

Name _____ Date _____

Unit 5 Review · · · · · · · · · · · · · · · · · · ·
Darken the circle for the word that best completes each analogy.

1. crust : bread :: cover : _____
   Ⓐ paper   Ⓑ butter   Ⓒ book

2. swimmer : pool :: runner : _____
   Ⓐ sport   Ⓑ track   Ⓒ relay

3. kind : nice :: tender : _____
   Ⓐ soft   Ⓑ hard   Ⓒ bright

4. bite : nibble :: fold : _____
   Ⓐ food   Ⓑ bend   Ⓒ handle

5. dentist : drill :: carpenter : _____
   Ⓐ hammer   Ⓑ teeth   Ⓒ builder

6. hurt : harm :: push : _____
   Ⓐ pull   Ⓑ help   Ⓒ shove

7. mane : horse :: wig : _____
   Ⓐ clown   Ⓑ hair   Ⓒ pony

8. firefighter : hose :: farmer : _____
   Ⓐ crop   Ⓑ field   Ⓒ hoe

TRY THIS Tell if the analogies describe parts of a whole, user and object, or synonyms.

Unit 5: Synonyms
Unlocking Analogies 2–3, SV 9781419033902
34
© Harcourt Achieve Inc. All rights reserved. www.harcourtschoolsupply.com

Answer Key

The **Answer Key** at the back of the book provides answers as well as explanations when needed.

· · · · · · · · · · · · · · Answer Key · · · · · · · · · · · · · ·

page 7
1. C (user/object)
2. A (name/description)
3. B (antonyms)
4. A (similar things)
5. C (synonyms)
6. B (parts of a whole)
7. A (parts of a whole)
8. B (user/object)

page 8
1. Cross out rectangle; add circle.
2. Cross out circle; add rectangle.
3. Cross out star; add triangle.
4. Cross out triangle; add star.

page 9
1. small hexagon
2. tilted rectangle
3. pyramid

page 10
1. small yield sign
2. small dog
3. big bowl

page 11
1. Cross out poodle; add shark. (fish)
2. Cross out pear; add parrot. (birds)
3. Cross out parrot; add pear. (fruit)
4. Cross out shark; add poodle. (dogs)

page 12
1. c, f
2. b, e
3. a, d

page 13
1. pen, crayon (write with)
2. peas, corn (vegetables)
3. spoon, knife (utensils)
4. shirt, pants (clothes)

page 14
1. Cross out plate. (printed materials)
2. Cross out river. (things to sit on)
3. Cross out sink. (types of shoes)
4. Cross out bench. (things to eat from)
5. Cross out slipper. (bodies of water)
6. Cross out journal. (appliances)

page 15
1. bed, pillow, dresser
2. oven, dishes, food
3. tub, toothbrush, towel

page 16
1. food
2. family
3. clothes
4. furniture
5. tools
6. sports

page 17
1. d
2. c
3. b
4. a
5. e

page 18
1.–6. Answers will vary.

page 19
1. horse
2. lunch
3. kitchen

page 20
1. A
2. C
3. C
4. B
5. A

page 21
1. swarm
2. bird
3. shovel
4. airport
5. year

page 22
1. C (similar things)
2. A (parts of a whole)
3. C (parts of a whole)
4. A (similar things)
5. B (similar things)
6. B (parts of a whole)
7. C (parts of a whole)
8. A (similar things)

page 23
1. a, d
2. c, f
3. e, h
4. b, g

page 24
1. Cross out glove; add saw.
2. Cross out microphone; add paintbrush.
3. Cross out paintbrush; add microphone.
4. Cross out saw; add glove.

page 25
1. pole
2. ship
3. bat
4. paintbrush

page 26
1. C
2. B
3. C
4. A
5. C

page 27
1. airplane
2. scissors
3. goal
4. clay
5. loom

www.harcourtschoolsupply.com
© Harcourt Achieve Inc. All rights reserved.
47
Answer Key
Unlocking Analogies 2–3, SV 9781419033902

Assessment ···■···■··■··■··■··■··■··■··

Darken the circle for the word that best completes each analogy.

1. <u>Swimmer</u> is to <u>pool</u> as <u>runner</u> is to _____.
   Ⓐ shoes   Ⓑ race   Ⓒ track

2. <u>Clown</u> is to <u>funny</u> as <u>monster</u> is to _____.
   Ⓐ scary   Ⓑ movie   Ⓒ giant

3. <u>Hard</u> is to <u>easy</u> as <u>tricky</u> is to _____.
   Ⓐ tough   Ⓑ simple   Ⓒ problem

4. <u>Daisy</u> is to <u>rose</u> as <u>apple</u> is to _____.
   Ⓐ pear   Ⓑ fruit   Ⓒ carrot

5. <u>Cold</u> is to <u>cool</u> as <u>hot</u> is to _____.
   Ⓐ fire   Ⓑ chilly   Ⓒ warm

6. <u>Tooth</u> is to <u>mouth</u> as <u>ear</u> is to _____.
   Ⓐ eyes   Ⓑ head   Ⓒ nose

7. <u>Wing</u> is to <u>bird</u> as <u>fin</u> is to _____.
   Ⓐ fish   Ⓑ fly   Ⓒ feather

8. <u>Writer</u> is to <u>book</u> as <u>artist</u> is to _____.
   Ⓐ library   Ⓑ painting   Ⓒ letter

Name _____   Date _____

Lesson I: The Right Shape ....

Shapes can belong to different groups.

Key to Solving

One of the shapes in this group doesn't belong.
Which shape doesn't belong?

The triangle doesn't belong in this group of circles.

Directions: Find the shape in each group that doesn't belong. Cross it out and then draw it in the group where it does belong.

1.	3.
2.	4.

Name the shapes in each group.

Unit 1: Shapes and Pictures
Unlocking Analogies 2–3, SV 9781419033902

Lesson 2: Shaping Up ··■··■··■··■··■··■··■··■··■··■·■·

An analogy is a way of comparing things. Analogies can be used to compare shapes.

Key to Solving

Look at these two shapes. How are they related?

They are both <u>circles</u>. One is big, and one is small.
Look at these two shapes. How are they related?

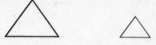

They are both <u>triangles</u>. One is big, and one is small.
An analogy can compare the four shapes.

 is to  is to

Directions: Circle the shape that completes the analogy.

1. ▭ is to ▭ as ⬡ is to	⬡ ▢
2. ▢ is to ◇ as ▭ is to	▭ ◹
3. ▢ is to ⬚(cube) as △ is to	◭ ▽

**Make your own analogy using shapes.
Trade with a classmate to solve.**

Name _____   Date _____

Lesson 3: Picture This ·····················

Analogies can be used to compare pictures.

Key to Solving

How are these pictures related?
They are both <u>apples</u>. One is big, and one is small.

How are these pictures related?
They are both <u>oranges</u>. One is big, and one is small.

You can use analogies to compare the four pictures.

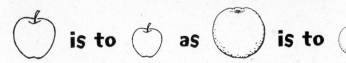
is to · · · is to as · · · is to · · · is to

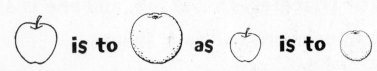
is to · · · as · · · is to

Directions: Circle the picture that completes the analogy.

1.	STOP is to STOP as YIELD is to	(traffic light) (YIELD)
2.	(cat) is to (dog) as (small cat) is to	(small dog) (cat)
3.	(cup) is to (large cup) as (bowl) is to	(large bowl) (cup)

TRY THIS

Make your own analogy using pictures.
Trade with a classmate to solve.

Unit 1: Shapes and Pictures
Unlocking Analogies 2–3, SV 9781419033902

· · · · · · ·
10

www.harcourtschoolsupply.com
© Harcourt Achieve Inc. All rights reserved.

Name _____   Date _____

Lesson 4: Grouping Pictures ....

Items in a group are alike in some way.

Key to Solving

One of the pictures in this group does not belong.
Which picture does not belong? How are the other
pictures in the group related?

The <u>carrot</u> does not belong to this group. An apple
and a banana are both <u>fruit</u>. A carrot is a <u>vegetable</u>.

Directions: Find the picture in each group that does
not belong. Cross it out and then write its name where
it does belong.

1.

_____

3.

_____

2.

_____

4.

_____

 TRY THIS **Tell what the pictures in
each group have in common.**

Unit 1: Shapes and Pictures
Unlocking Analogies 2–3, SV 9781419033902

Name _____   Date _____

Lesson 5: Making Groups ••••••••••••••••••

Things that are alike can be put into the same group.

Key to Solving

What groups can you make?

Puppy and goldfish are <u>animals</u> or <u>pets</u>.

Doll and truck are <u>toys</u>.

Banana and apple are types of <u>fruit</u>.

Directions: Each picture on the right goes in one group on the left. Find the group that each picture belongs to and write the letter of the picture on the correct line.

1. School Supplies

   ___ ___ ___

2. Clothes

   ___ ___

3. Tools

   ___

a.   b.

c.   d.

e.   f.

Name something else that goes in each group.

Lesson 6: Joining Groups ·•··•··•··•··•··•·

A group is made up of things that are alike.

Key to Solving

How are these things alike?

A truck, a bicycle, and a car all have wheels.

Directions: Look at the pictures on the left. Find two pictures on the right that belong to the same group. Write their names on the correct lines.

1.

   _____   _____

2.

   _____   _____

3.

   _____   _____

4.

   _____   _____

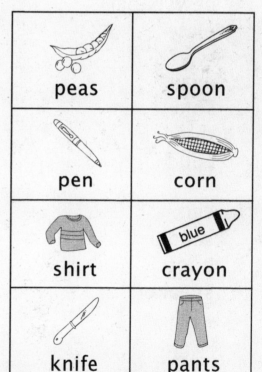

peas	spoon
pen	corn
shirt	crayon
knife	pants

 Write the name of each group next to it.

Name _____   Date _____

Lesson 7: The Right Group ·············

Things that are alike belong to the same group.

Key to Solving

Which of these things does not belong?

parrot   swan   mouse   robin   goose

Parrot, swan, robin, and goose are all <u>birds</u>. A <u>mouse</u> does not belong to this group.

Directions: Cross out each thing that does not belong.

1. book
   magazine
   newspaper
   plate

2. chair
   sofa
   river
   couch

3. sink
   sandal
   boot
   sneaker

4. dish
   bowl
   platter
   bench

5. lake
   slipper
   pond
   sea

6. toaster
   dishwasher
   journal
   oven

TRY THIS   **Find the group for the words you crossed out.**

·········

Unit 2: Similarities
Unlocking Analogies 2–3, SV 9781419033902   www.harcourtschoolsupply.com

Name _____ Date _____

Lesson 8: The Right Place

Things that are alike can be found in the same place.

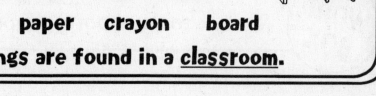

Key to Solving

Where are all of these things found?

desk   pencil   paper   crayon   board

All of these things are found in a classroom.

Directions: Write the words from the box under the word that tells where each thing would be found.

WORD BOX

| tub | bed | oven | toothbrush | pillow |
| dishes | dresser | towel | food |

1. Bedroom   **2. Kitchen**   **3. Bathroom**

_____   _____   _____

_____   _____   _____

_____   _____   _____

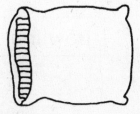   

List two more things that are found in each place.

Unit 2: Similarities
Unlocking Analogies 2–3, SV 9781419033902

Name _____ Date _____

Unit 2 Review ⋯⋯⋯⋯⋯⋯⋯⋯⋯⋯⋯⋯

The words in each word web name things in a group.
Choose a word from the box that describes the group.
Write the word to finish the web.

 **WORD BOX**   family   tools   sports   food   furniture   clothes

1.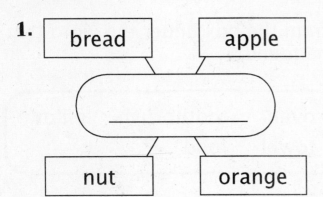
bread   apple
_____
nut   orange

4.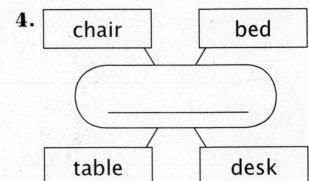
chair   bed
_____
table   desk

2.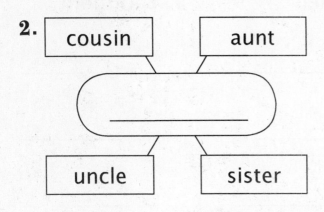
cousin   aunt
_____
uncle   sister

5.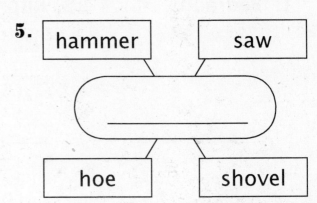
hammer   saw
_____
hoe   shovel

3.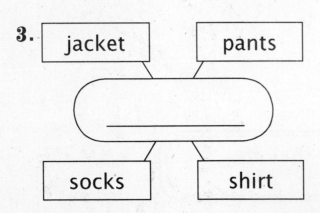
jacket   pants
_____
socks   shirt

6.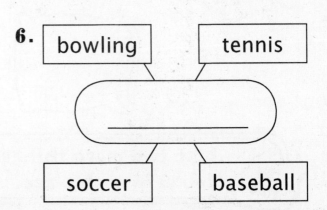
bowling   tennis
_____
soccer   baseball

Unit 2: Similarities
Unlocking Analogies 2–3, SV 9781419033902

Lesson 9: Parts of a Whole

A whole object can be divided into parts.

Key to Solving

What do these parts make up?

Eye, ear, mouth, and nose are all parts of a <u>face</u>.

Directions: Write the letter of the part next to the whole.

_____ 1.   a.

_____ 2.   b.

_____ 3.   c.

_____ 4.   d.

_____ 5.    e.

TRY THIS   **Name another part that goes with each whole.**

Name _____ Date _____

Lesson 10: Picking Parts ·····················

Parts can be used to describe a whole.

Key to Solving

What parts make up a horse?

Hooves, a mane, and a tail are all parts of a <u>horse</u>.

Directions: Write three parts of each whole.

1.

_____ _____ _____

2.

_____ _____ _____

3.

_____ _____ _____

4.

_____ _____ _____

5.

_____ _____ _____

TRY THIS

Draw a picture of an object and trade with a classmate to name the parts of a whole.

Name _____ Date _____

Lesson II: Comparing Parts

Analogies can be used to compare parts of things.

Key to Solving

How are these parts and wholes related?

A <u>finger</u> is part of a <u>hand</u>, and a <u>toe</u> is part of a <u>foot</u>.

You can make an analogy to compare parts of different wholes.

<u>Hand</u> is to <u>finger</u> as <u>foot</u> is to <u>toe</u>.

Directions: Write the word from the box that best completes each sentence.

WORD BOX

kitchen   bird   horse   lunch   painting

1. A <u>paw</u> is part of a <u>dog</u>, and a <u>hoof</u> is part of a

   _____.

2. <u>Cereal</u> is part of <u>breakfast</u>, and a <u>sandwich</u> is part of

   _____.

3. A <u>desk</u> is part of a <u>classroom</u>, and a <u>stove</u> is part of a

   _____.

TRY THIS

Name another part for each whole listed above.

Unit 3: Part to Whole
Unlocking Analogies 2–3, SV 9781419033902

Name _____ Date _____

Lesson 12: Parts in Pairs ⋅⋅⋅⋅⋅⋅⋅⋅⋅⋅⋅⋅⋅⋅⋅⋅⋅⋅⋅

Analogies can be used to compare parts of one thing to parts of another.

Key to Solving

How are these words related?

fish   school   bird   flock

A <u>fish</u> is part of a <u>school</u>. A <u>bird</u> is part of a <u>flock</u>.

<u>Fish</u> is to <u>school</u> as <u>bird</u> is to <u>flock</u>.

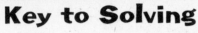

Directions: Read the first word pair. Then darken the circle for the word that best completes the second word pair.

1. A <u>flower</u> is part of a <u>garden</u>, and a <u>tree</u> is part of a _____.
   Ⓐ forest   Ⓑ oak   Ⓒ leaf

2. A <u>cow</u> is part of a <u>herd</u>, and a <u>wolf</u> is part of a _____.
   Ⓐ paw   Ⓑ dog   Ⓒ pack

3. <u>Lettuce</u> is part of a <u>salad</u>, and <u>bread</u> is part of a _____.
   Ⓐ plate   Ⓑ pan   Ⓒ sandwich

4. An <u>eye</u> is part of a <u>face</u>, and a <u>knee</u> is part of a _____.
   Ⓐ foot   Ⓑ leg   Ⓒ kick

5. A <u>drum</u> is part of a <u>band</u>, and a <u>chapter</u> is part of a _____.
   Ⓐ book   Ⓑ page   Ⓒ paper

TRY THIS

Read your answers to a partner. Explain why you chose the words you did.

Lesson 13: Parts in Analogies ....

Analogies can be used to compare parts to wholes.

Key to Solving

Another way of reading an analogy is with special symbols. Look at the analogy below.

cow : herd :: dog : pack

The single colon (:) compares two items in a word pair. The double colon (::) compares the first word pair to the second.

Read the analogy as "<u>Cow</u> is to <u>herd</u> as <u>dog</u> is to <u>pack</u>."

Directions: Write a word from the box to complete each analogy.

WORD BOX

| forest | bird | year | shovel | swarm | airport |

1. goose : flock :: bee : _____

2. trunk : elephant :: beak : _____

3. handle : broom :: blade : _____

4. barn : farm :: airplane : _____

5. day : week :: month : _____

TRY THIS

Read each analogy out loud to a partner. For the colon symbol :, say "is to." For the double colon symbol ::, say "as."

Unit 3 Review ·■··■··■··■··■··■··■··■··■·.

Darken the circle for the word that best completes
each analogy.

1. Car is to truck as canoe is to _____.

  Ⓐ water   Ⓑ oar   Ⓒ sailboat

2. Thread is to shirt as yarn is to _____.

  Ⓐ blanket   Ⓑ sewing   Ⓒ ball

3. Cheese is to pizza as flour is to _____.

  Ⓐ stone   Ⓑ bake   Ⓒ bread

4. Mother is to father as sister is to _____.

  Ⓐ brother   Ⓑ friend   Ⓒ teacher

5. Bee is to ant as frog is to _____.

  Ⓐ hop   Ⓑ toad   Ⓒ fly

6. Stem is to plant as trunk is to _____.

  Ⓐ field   Ⓑ tree   Ⓒ farmer

7. Fur is to animal as hair is to _____.

  Ⓐ head   Ⓑ brush   Ⓒ human

8. Grape is to pear as milk is to _____.

  Ⓐ juice   Ⓑ buy   Ⓒ glass

**Tell if the analogies describe things
that go together or parts of a whole.**

Name _____ Date _____

Lesson 14: Tools People Use ....

People use tools to do different things.

Key to Solving

Which tool would a <u>farmer</u> use?

A <u>farmer</u> would use a <u>pitchfork</u>.

A <u>cook</u> would use a <u>pot</u>.

<u>Farmer</u> is to <u>pitchfork</u> as <u>cook</u> is to <u>pot</u>.

Directions: Find two tools that each person would use. Write the letters on the correct lines.

1.   _____ _____

2.   _____ _____

3.   _____ _____

4.   _____ _____

a. 	b.
c. 	d.
e. 	f.
g. 	h. 

Think of another tool that each person uses.

Unlocking Analogies 2–3, SV 9781419033902

Name _____ Date _____

Lesson 15: The Right Tool

People use different tools for different jobs.

Key to Solving

A firefighter uses tools to do his or her job. Which tool below would a firefighter not use?

A firefighter would not use a baseball.

Directions: Find the tool in each group that does not belong. Cross it out and then draw it in the group where it does belong.

1.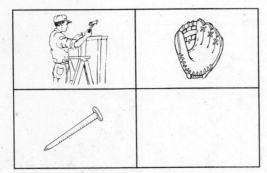

2.

3.

4.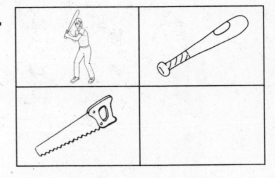

 Name another tool that each person uses.

Name _____   Date _____

Lesson 16: Comparing Tools ·············

Analogies can compare tools and the people who use them.

Key to Solving

How are these tools and their users related?

A <u>carpenter</u> uses a <u>saw</u>, and a <u>baker</u> uses a <u>bowl</u>.

You can make an analogy to compare tools and their users.

<u>Carpenter</u> is to <u>saw</u> as <u>baker</u> is to <u>bowl</u>.

Directions: Write the word from the box that best completes each sentence.

WORD BOX   ship   paintbrush   bat   pole

1. A <u>surfer</u> uses a <u>surfboard</u>, and a <u>fisher</u> uses a _____.

2. A <u>driver</u> uses a <u>truck</u>, and a <u>sailor</u> uses a _____.

3. A <u>golfer</u> uses a <u>club</u>, and a <u>baseball player</u> uses

   a _____.

4. A <u>writer</u> uses a <u>pen</u>, and an <u>artist</u> uses a _____.

TRY THIS   Make your own analogy about two people and the tools they use.

·· ·· ·· ··

Unit 4: User to Object
Unlocking Analogies 2–3, SV 9781419033902

Name _____   Date _____

Lesson 17: Tools in Pairs ·····················

Analogies can compare one user and tool to another user and tool.

Key to Solving

How are these words related?

swimmer   swimsuit   runner   shorts

A <u>swimmer</u> uses a <u>swimsuit</u>. A <u>runner</u> uses <u>shorts</u>.

<u>Swimmer</u> is to <u>swimsuit</u> as <u>runner</u> is to <u>shorts</u>.

Directions: Read the first word pair. Then darken the circle for the word that best completes the second word pair.

1. <u>Bicycle rider</u> is to <u>bike</u> as <u>skater</u> is to _____.
   Ⓐ ice   Ⓑ sneakers   Ⓒ skates

2. <u>Baby</u> is to <u>bottle</u> as <u>child</u> is to _____.
   Ⓐ house   Ⓑ cup   Ⓒ book

3. <u>Farmer</u> is to <u>tractor</u> as <u>captain</u> is to _____.
   Ⓐ sea   Ⓑ truck   Ⓒ ship

4. <u>Actor</u> is to <u>costume</u> as <u>police officer</u> is to _____.
   Ⓐ uniform   Ⓑ stage   Ⓒ road

5. <u>Pilot</u> is to <u>plane</u> as <u>plumber</u> is to _____.
   Ⓐ wing   Ⓑ wheel   Ⓒ pipe

Choose two analogies above and rewrite them in symbol form.

Lesson 18: Tools in Analogies ⋯⋯⋯⋯⋯

Analogies can compare tools and their users.

Key to Solving

Another way of reading an analogy is with special symbols. Look at the analogy below.

writer : pen :: artist : paintbrush

The single colon (:) compares two items in a word pair. The double colon (::) compares the first word pair to the second.

Read the analogy as "<u>Writer</u> is to <u>pen</u> as <u>artist</u> is to <u>paintbrush</u>."

Directions: Write a word from the box to complete each analogy.

WORD BOX   mask   goal   loom   airplane   clay   scissors

1. driver : car :: pilot : _____

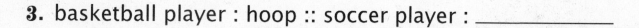

2. carpenter : hammer :: barber : _____

3. basketball player : hoop :: soccer player : _____

4. baker : flour :: potter : _____

5. cowboy : lasso :: weaver : _____

TRY THIS   Read each analogy above to a partner.

Unlocking Analogies 2–3, SV 9781419033902

Name _____   Date _____

Unit 4 Review ··•··•··■··•··■··•··■··•··■··•··■··•·

Darken the circle for the word that best completes each
analogy.

1. <u>Baseball player</u> is to <u>cap</u> as <u>football player</u> is to ____.
   Ⓐ field   Ⓑ team   Ⓒ helmet

2. <u>Carrot</u> is to <u>lettuce</u> as <u>banana</u> is to ____.
   Ⓐ apple   Ⓑ peel   Ⓒ yellow

3. <u>Ear</u> is to <u>face</u> as <u>shoelace</u> is to ____.
   Ⓐ head   Ⓑ sneaker   Ⓒ walking

4. <u>Duck</u> is to <u>swan</u> as <u>lion</u> is to ____.
   Ⓐ goose   Ⓑ hungry   Ⓒ tiger

5. <u>Number</u> is to <u>clock</u> as <u>letter</u> is to ____.
   Ⓐ sign   Ⓑ crayon   Ⓒ time

6. <u>Teacher</u> is to <u>classroom</u> as <u>worker</u> is to ____.
   Ⓐ job   Ⓑ busy   Ⓒ office

7. <u>Letter carrier</u> is to <u>mailbag</u> as <u>scientist</u> is to ____.
   Ⓐ insect   Ⓑ microscope   Ⓒ doctor

8. <u>Goldfish</u> is to <u>whale</u> as <u>wren</u> is to ____.
   Ⓐ hawk   Ⓑ catfish   Ⓒ nest

TRY THIS

Tell if the analogies describe things that go together, parts of a whole, or user and object.

··■··•··■··

28

Name _____ Date _____

Lesson 19: What Are Synonyms? ·········

Synonyms are words that mean almost the same thing.

Key to Solving

Which words mean the same thing?

   smile   cry   grin

<u>Smile</u> and <u>grin</u> mean the same thing.
They are synonyms.

Directions: Draw lines to match the synonyms.

1. town   leave

2. street   city

3. go   correct

4. begin   sick

5. ill   road

6. right   start

Think of another synonym pair.

Name _____ Date _____

Lesson 20: Matched Pairs

Synonyms are words that mean almost the same thing.

Key to Solving

Which two words name this picture?

pants   socks   jeans

<u>Pants</u> and <u>jeans</u> name this picture.

They are synonyms.

Directions: Write two synonyms from the box for each picture.

WORD BOX

boat	chicken	seat	car	lad	hen
boy	auto	gift	ship	present	chair

1.  _____
_____

4. _____
_____

2. _____
_____

5. _____
_____

3. _____
_____

6. _____
_____

 Think of another synonym for each pair.

Name _____ Date _____

Lesson 21: Similar Words  ·■·■··■··■··■·■·■··■··

When two words mean the same thing, they are
called synonyms.

Key to Solving

Which words below are synonyms?

   hot   cold   warm   chilly

You can make word pairs of synonyms:
hot—warm, cold—chilly.

Directions: Write the letter of the correct synonym from the
right side next to each word on the left.

_____ **1.** fast   **a.** nice

_____ **2.** quit   **b.** noisy

_____ **3.** polite   **c.** quick

_____ **4.** loud   **d.** mad

_____ **5.** angry   **e.** fearless

_____ **6.** brave   **f.** stop

 **Name a third synonym that
goes with each pair.**

www.harcourtschoolsupply.com
© Harcourt Achieve Inc. All rights reserved.

Unit 5: Synonyms
Unlocking Analogies 2–3, SV 9781419033902

Name _____ Date _____

Lesson 22: Picking Synonyms ⋯⋯⋯⋯⋯⋯

Analogies can be used to compare pairs of synonyms.

Key to Solving

How can you compare two word pairs of synonyms?

small, little   big, large

You can make an analogy to compare word pairs.

<u>Small</u> is to <u>little</u> as <u>big</u> is to <u>large</u>.

Directions: Darken the circle for the word that best completes each analogy.

1. <u>Happy</u> is to <u>glad</u> as <u>unhappy</u> is to _____.
   Ⓐ angry   Ⓑ cheerful   Ⓒ sad

2. <u>Hop</u> is to <u>jump</u> as <u>walk</u> is to _____.
   Ⓐ run   Ⓑ stroll   Ⓒ jog

3. <u>Ocean</u> is to <u>sea</u> as <u>field</u> is to _____.
   Ⓐ meadow   Ⓑ mountain   Ⓒ play

4. <u>Smell</u> is to <u>sniff</u> as <u>see</u> is to _____.
   Ⓐ nose   Ⓑ eat   Ⓒ look

5. <u>Cup</u> is to <u>mug</u> as <u>plate</u> is to _____.
   Ⓐ dinner   Ⓑ dish   Ⓒ bowl

TRY THIS

Create your own synonym word pairs. Trade with a partner and think of a third word to go in each pair.

Name _____   Date _____

Lesson 23: Synonyms in Analogies ·········

Analogies can be used to compare synonyms.

Key to Solving

How do you read the symbols used in analogies?

  wet : damp :: high : tall

The single colon (:) compares two items in a word pair. The double colon (::) compares the first word pair to the second.

<u>Wet</u> is to <u>damp</u> as <u>high</u> is to <u>tall</u>.

Directions: Write a word from the box to complete each analogy.

WORD BOX   calm   simple   nasty   dark   silky   neat

1. sunny : bright :: cloudy : _____

2. dirty : messy :: clean : _____

3. windy : breezy :: still : _____

4. friendly : nice :: mean : _____

5. hard : tough :: easy : _____

6. sticky : gummy :: smooth : _____

Read each analogy aloud to a partner.

Unit 5: Synonyms
Unlocking Analogies 2–3, SV 9781419033902

Name _____ Date _____

Unit 5 Review ....

Darken the circle for the word that best completes each analogy.

1. crust : bread :: cover : ____
   Ⓐ paper   Ⓑ butter   Ⓒ book

2. swimmer : pool :: runner : ____
   Ⓐ sport   Ⓑ track   Ⓒ relay

3. kind : nice :: tender : ____
   Ⓐ soft   Ⓑ hard   Ⓒ bright

4. bite : nibble :: fold : ____
   Ⓐ food   Ⓑ bend   Ⓒ handle

5. dentist : drill :: carpenter : ____
   Ⓐ hammer   Ⓑ teeth   Ⓒ builder

6. hurt : harm :: push : ____
   Ⓐ pull   Ⓑ help   Ⓒ shove

7. mane : horse :: wig : ____
   Ⓐ clown   Ⓑ hair   Ⓒ pony

8. firefighter : hose :: farmer : ____
   Ⓐ crop   Ⓑ field   Ⓒ hoe

TRY THIS   **Tell if the analogies describe parts of a whole, user and object, or synonyms.**

Name _____ Date _____

Lesson 24: What Are Antonyms? ....

Antonyms are words that mean the opposite of each other.

Key to Solving

Which pictures show opposite things?

One boy is <u>smiling</u>, and one boy is <u>frowning</u>.
<u>Smiling</u> and <u>frowning</u> are antonyms.

Directions: Look at the pictures on the left. Find the pictures on the right that show the opposite. Write the letter of each picture on the correct line.

____ 1.   **a.**

____ 2.    **b.**

____ 3.   **c.**

____ 4.   **d.**

                                      e.

____ 5.

TRY THIS   **Tell how the pictures in each group are different.**

_____

Unit 6: Antonyms
Unlocking Analogies 2–3, SV 9781419033902

Name _____ Date _____

Lesson 25: Opposites Attract

Antonyms are words that mean the opposite of each other.

Key to Solving

Which of these pictures shows the opposite of <u>girl</u>?

The second picture shows a <u>boy</u>. <u>Boy</u> is the opposite of <u>girl</u>.

<u>Boy</u> and <u>girl</u> are antonyms.

Directions: Draw lines to match the antonym pairs.

1. large   close

2. open   dry

3. back   downstairs

4. wet   small

5. upstairs   cry

6. laugh   front

 Think of another antonym pair.

Unit 6: Antonyms
Unlocking Analogies 2–3, SV 9781419033902

www.harcourtschoolsupply.com

Lesson 26: Opposite Words ....

When two words are opposites, they are called antonyms.

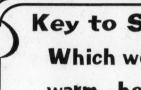

Key to Solving

Which words below are antonyms?
warm hot cold chilly
You can make word pairs of antonyms:
<u>warm—chilly</u>, <u>hot—cold</u>.

Directions: Write the letter of the correct antonym from the right side next to each word on the left.

_____	1. slow	**a.**	short
_____	2. work	**b.**	melt
_____	3. tall	**c.**	play
_____	4. freeze	**d.**	quiet
_____	5. noisy	**e.**	float
_____	6. sink	**f.**	fast

Think of another antonym for each word on the left side.

Lesson 27: Picking Antonyms  ·····················

Analogies can be used to compare pairs of antonyms.

Key to Solving

How can you compare two word pairs of antonyms?

  tiny, huge   small, large

You can make an analogy to compare word pairs.

Tiny is to huge as small is to large.

Directions: Darken the circle for the word that best completes each analogy.

1. Quiet is to loud as hard is to _____.
   Ⓐ soft   Ⓑ still   Ⓒ noisy

2. Up is to down as left is to _____.
   Ⓐ right   Ⓑ above   Ⓒ behind

3. Day is to night as morning is to _____.
   Ⓐ sunrise   Ⓑ evening   Ⓒ breakfast

4. Thick is to thin as broad is to _____.
   Ⓐ narrow   Ⓑ wide   Ⓒ big

5. Sick is to well as ill is to _____.
   Ⓐ pale   Ⓑ hospital   Ⓒ healthy

Create your own antonym word pairs.
Trade with a partner and think of a
different antonym to go in each pair.

····················
38

Lesson 28: Antonyms in Analogies ·······

Analogies can be used to compare antonyms.

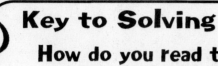

Key to Solving

How do you read the symbols used in analogies?

dark : light :: night : day

The single colon (:) compares two items in a word pair.

The double colon (::) compares the first word pair to the second.

<u>Dark</u> is to <u>light</u> as <u>night</u> is to <u>day</u>.

Directions: Write a word from the box to complete each analogy.

WORD BOX

wonderful   front   take   winter   stranger   poor

1. win : lose :: give : _____

2. friend : enemy :: buddy : _____

3. sweet : sour :: rich : _____

4. noon : midnight :: summer : _____

5. top : bottom :: back : _____

6. bad : good :: awful : _____

 TRY THIS   **Read each analogy aloud to a partner.**

Unit 6 Review ··

Darken the circle for the word that best completes each analogy.

1. glass : cup :: plate : _____

   Ⓐ dish   Ⓑ fork   Ⓒ table

2. wheel : truck :: sail : _____

   Ⓐ oar   Ⓑ water   Ⓒ boat

3. buy : sell :: break : _____

   Ⓐ fix   Ⓑ money   Ⓒ angry

4. sleeve : shirt :: lock : _____

   Ⓐ door   Ⓑ clock   Ⓒ hat

5. singer : voice :: printer : _____

   Ⓐ ink   Ⓑ hammer   Ⓒ song

6. narrow : wide :: tall : _____

   Ⓐ high   Ⓑ short   Ⓒ broad

7. rock : stone :: story : _____

   Ⓐ tale   Ⓑ poem   Ⓒ song

8. light : dark :: white : _____

   Ⓐ bright   Ⓑ hot   Ⓒ black

Tell if the analogies describe parts of a whole, user and object, synonyms, or antonyms.

Name _____ Date _____

Lesson 29: What's It Like? ⋯⋯⋯⋯⋯⋯

Adjectives are used to describe things.

Key to Solving

How would you describe these pictures?

The <u>kitten</u> is <u>furry</u>, and the <u>lamb</u> is <u>woolly</u>.

You can make an analogy to compare the pictures.

<u>Kitten</u> is to <u>furry</u> as <u>lamb</u> is to <u>woolly</u>.

Directions: Write the word from the box that describes the picture.

WORD BOX   icy   sharp   fast   yellow   slow   hot

1.   _____

2.   _____

3.   _____

4.   _____

5.   _____

6.  _____

TRY THIS   **Think of another word to describe each picture.**

Unit 7: Name and Description
Unlocking Analogies 2–3, SV 9781419033902

Lesson 30: Describe It!

Nouns are described with adjectives.

Key to Solving

How can you describe the pictures shown below?

The basketball, globe, and orange are all <u>round</u>.

Directions: Each picture below goes with one describing word. Write the letter of each picture on the correct line.

1. large

   ____ ____

2. sticky

   ____ ____

3. striped

   ____ ____

a. 	**b.** 
c. 	**d.** 
e. 	**f.** 

 Name something else that goes with each description above.

Name _____ Date _____

Lesson 31: Names and Descriptions ....

Descriptions can tell what is special about something.

Key to Solving

Which words below go together?
turtle   rabbit   slow   quick

A <u>turtle</u> is <u>slow</u>, and a <u>rabbit</u> is <u>quick</u>.

You can make word pairs of names and descriptions:
<u>turtle—slow</u>, <u>rabbit—quick</u>.

Directions: Write the letter of the correct describing word from the right side next to each word on the left.

_____ 1. carrot   **a.** square

_____ 2. field   **b.** shaggy

_____ 3. box   **c.** crisp

_____ 4. lemon   **d.** sandy

_____ 5. sheepdog   **e.** grassy

_____ 6. beach   **f.** sour

Think of another word to describe each word on the left side.

Unlocking Analogies 2–3, SV 9781419033902

Lesson 32: Picking Descriptions ···········

Analogies can be used to compare names and descriptions.

Key to Solving

How can you compare names and descriptions?
chick, downy   toad, bumpy
You can make an analogy to compare word pairs.
Chick is to downy as toad is to bumpy.

Directions: Darken the circle for the word that best completes each analogy.

1. <u>Puppy</u> is to <u>playful</u> as <u>mouse</u> is to _____.
   Ⓐ sad   Ⓑ quiet   Ⓒ rat

2. <u>Pillow</u> is to <u>soft</u> as <u>rock</u> is to _____.
   Ⓐ stone   Ⓑ white   Ⓒ hard

3. <u>Gum</u> is to <u>sticky</u> as <u>apple</u> is to _____.
   Ⓐ tree   Ⓑ crunchy   Ⓒ pear

4. <u>Ladybug</u> is to <u>red</u> as <u>grasshopper</u> is to _____.
   Ⓐ green   Ⓑ hop   Ⓒ insect

5. <u>Pin</u> is to <u>sharp</u> as <u>marble</u> is to _____.
   Ⓐ flat   Ⓑ game   Ⓒ round

 Make your own word pair and trade with a partner to form an analogy.

Lesson 33: Descriptions in Analogies ......

Analogies can be used to compare names and descriptions.

Key to Solving

How do you read the symbols used in analogies?

   fire : hot :: ice : cold

The single colon (:) compares two items in a word pair.

The double colon (::) compares the first word pair to the second.

   <u>Fire</u> is to <u>hot</u> as <u>ice</u> is to <u>cold</u>.

Directions: Write a word from the box to complete each analogy.

WORD BOX   tiny   dry   hard   sour   yellow   low

1. attic : high :: basement : _____

2. popcorn : salty :: pickle : _____

3. giraffe : tall :: ant : _____

4. lettuce : green :: corn : _____

5. scissors : sharp :: hammer : _____

   Read each analogy aloud to a partner.

Unit 7 Review ·····················

Darken the circle for the word that best completes each analogy.

1. cap : hat :: sandal : ____
   Ⓐ shorts   Ⓑ strap   Ⓒ shoe

2. miner : pick :: logger : ____
   Ⓐ driver   Ⓑ tree   Ⓒ ax

3. glue : sticky :: sheep : ____
   Ⓐ woolly   Ⓑ old   Ⓒ gummy

4. tooth : mouth :: finger : ____
   Ⓐ thumb   Ⓑ nail   Ⓒ hand

5. whisper : shout :: mumble : ____
   Ⓐ chat   Ⓑ yell   Ⓒ sigh

6. pail : bucket :: pot : ____
   Ⓐ pan   Ⓑ soup   Ⓒ stove

7. grocer : food :: banker : ____
   Ⓐ teller   Ⓑ money   Ⓒ store

8. skyscraper : tall :: snow : ____
   Ⓐ wooden   Ⓑ giant   Ⓒ cold

TRY THIS **Tell if the analogies describe parts of a whole, user and object, synonyms, antonyms, or name/description.**

·-·-·-·-·-·

page 7
1. C (user/object)
2. A (name/description)
3. B (antonyms)
4. A (similar things)
5. C (synonyms)
6. B (parts of a whole)
7. A (parts of a whole)
8. B (user/object)

page 8
1. Cross out rectangle; add circle.
2. Cross out circle; add rectangle.
3. Cross out star; add triangle.
4. Cross out triangle; add star.

page 9
1. small hexagon
2. tilted rectangle
3. pyramid

page 10
1. small yield sign
2. small dog
3. big bowl

page 11
1. Cross out poodle; add shark. (fish)
2. Cross out pear; add parrot. (birds)
3. Cross out parrot; add pear. (fruit)
4. Cross out shark; add poodle. (dogs)

page 12
1. c, f
2. b, e
3. a, d

page 13
1. pen, crayon (write with)
2. peas, corn (vegetables)
3. spoon, knife (utensils)
4. shirt, pants (clothes)

page 14
1. Cross out plate. (printed materials)
2. Cross out river. (things to sit on)
3. Cross out sink. (types of shoes)
4. Cross out bench. (things to eat from)
5. Cross out slipper. (bodies of water)
6. Cross out journal. (appliances)

page 15
1. bed, pillow, dresser
2. oven, dishes, food
3. tub, toothbrush, towel

page 16
1. food
2. family
3. clothes
4. furniture
5. tools
6. sports

page 17
1. d
2. c
3. b
4. a
5. e

page 18
1.–5. Answers will vary.

page 19
1. horse
2. lunch
3. kitchen

page 20
1. A
2. C
3. C
4. B
5. A

page 21
1. swarm
2. bird
3. shovel
4. airport
5. year

page 22
1. C (similar things)
2. A (parts of a whole)
3. C (parts of a whole)
4. A (similar things)
5. B (similar things)
6. B (parts of a whole)
7. C (parts of a whole)
8. A (similar things)

page 23
1. a, d
2. c, f
3. e, h
4. b, g

page 24
1. Cross out glove; add saw.
2. Cross out microphone; add paintbrush.
3. Cross out paintbrush; add microphone.
4. Cross out saw; add glove.

page 25
1. pole
2. ship
3. bat
4. paintbrush

page 26
1. C
2. B
3. C
4. A
5. C

page 27
1. airplane
2. scissors
3. goal
4. clay
5. loom

Answer Key

Unlocking Analogies 2–3, SV 9781419033902

page 28

1. C (user/object)
2. A (similar things)
3. B (parts of a whole)
4. C (similar things)
5. A (parts of a whole)
6. C (user/object)
7. B (user/object)
8. A (similar things)

page 29

1. town, city
2. street, road
3. go, leave
4. begin, start
5. ill, sick
6. right, correct

page 30

1. boat, ship
2. car, auto
3. seat, chair
4. chicken, hen
5. boy, lad
6. gift, present

page 31

1. c
2. f
3. a
4. b
5. d
6. e

page 32

1. C
2. B
3. A
4. C
5. B

page 33

1. dark
2. neat
3. calm
4. nasty
5. simple
6. silky

page 34

1. C (parts of a whole)
2. B (user/object)
3. A (synonyms)
4. B (synonyms)
5. A (user/object)
6. C (synonyms)
7. A (parts of a whole)
8. C (user/object)

page 35

1. a
2. d
3. e
4. c
5. b

page 36

1. large, small
2. open, close
3. back, front
4. wet, dry
5. upstairs, downstairs
6. laugh, cry

page 37

1. f
2. c
3. a
4. b
5. d
6. e

page 38

1. A
2. A
3. B
4. A
5. C

page 39

1. take
2. stranger
3. poor
4. winter
5. front
6. wonderful

page 40

1. A (synonyms)
2. C (parts of a whole)
3. A (antonyms)
4. A (parts of a whole)
5. A (user/object)
6. B (antonyms)
7. A (synonyms)
8. C (antonyms)

page 41

1. hot
2. icy
3. slow
4. sharp
5. yellow
6. fast

page 42

1. d, e
2. a, f
3. b, c

page 43

1. c
2. e
3. a
4. f
5. b
6. d

page 44

1. B
2. C
3. B
4. A
5. C

page 45

1. low
2. sour
3. tiny
4. yellow
5. hard

page 46

1. C (synonyms)
2. C (user/object)
3. A (name/description)
4. C (parts of a whole)
5. B (antonyms)
6. A (synonyms)
7. B (user/object)
8. C (name/description)